Poems in Spectacle & Pigsty were
selected from the following books:

『川萎え』(1987)
Riverwilt

『反復彷徨』(1992)
Wheeling Adrift

『特性のない陽のもとに』(1993)
Under the Rising Sun Without Character

『アダージェット、暗澹と』(1996)
Adagietto in Gloom

『幸福な物質』(2002)
Felicitous Substance

『ニューインスピレーション』(2003)
New Inspiration

『街の衣のいちまい下の虹は蛇だ』(2005)
One Layer Below the City's Slough, There's a Rainbow, Snake

『スペクタクル』(2006)
Spectacle

『稲妻狩』(2007)
Lightning Excursion

『plan14』(2007)
plan 14

『言葉たちは芝居をつづけよ、つまり移動を、移動を』(2008)
Words, Carry on Their Performance, Migrating, Migrating

Spectacle & Pigsty

Spectacle & Pigsty

Selected Poems of
Kiwao Nomura

Translated by
Kyoko Yoshida
&
Forrest Gander

OMNIDAWN PUBLISHING
RICHMOND, CALIFORNIA
2011

Cover Art: *Lichen Masks* by K. Ruby Blume
Ceramic, photograph by K. Ruby Blume

Book cover and interior design by Ken Keegan

Offset printed in the United States on archival, acid-free recycled paper
by Thomson-Shore, Inc., Dexter, Michigan

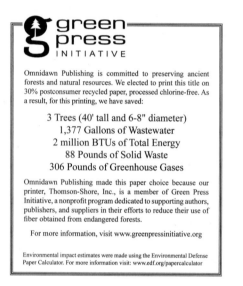

green press
INITIATIVE

Omnidawn Publishing is committed to preserving ancient
forests and natural resources. We elected to print this title on
30% postconsumer recycled paper, processed chlorine-free. As
a result, for this printing, we have saved:

3 Trees (40' tall and 6-8" diameter)
1,377 Gallons of Wastewater
2 million BTUs of Total Energy
88 Pounds of Solid Waste
306 Pounds of Greenhouse Gases

Omnidawn Publishing made this paper choice because our
printer, Thomson-Shore, Inc., is a member of Green Press
Initiative, a nonprofit program dedicated to supporting authors,
publishers, and suppliers in their efforts to reduce their use of
fiber obtained from endangered forests.

For more information, visit www.greenpressinitiative.org

Environmental impact estimates were made using the Environmental Defense
Paper Calculator. For more information visit: www.edf.org/papercalculator

Library of Congress Catalog-in-Publication Data

Nomura, Kiwao.
  [Poems. English. Selections]
  Spectacle & pigsty : selected poems of Kiwao Nomura / translated by
    Kyoko Yoshida & Forrest Gander.
    p. cm.
  ISBN 978-1-890650-53-7 (pbk. : alk. paper)
  I. Yoshida, Kyoko, 1969- II. Gander, Forrest, 1956- III. Title.
  PL857.O46A2 2011
  895.6'15--dc23

                            2011026857

Published by Omnidawn Publishing, Richmond, California
www.omnidawn.com   (510) 237-5472   (800) 792-4957
        10 9 8 7 6 5 4 3 2 1
            ISBN: 978-1-890650-53-7

Acknowledgements

Grateful acknowledgements to the editors of the following journals where many of these poems were first published:

91st Meridian, "Barely Hinged," "(scattering dust, we go crazy)" and "(and when I embraced you), Spring 2010"

Alligatorzine (Belgium), "Romance," "(one day suddenly)," "Eyeground Road"

Asymptote Journal (Taiwan), "On Prose," Winter 2010

Colorado Review, Sections 1-3 of "On the Way to the Site of Doppo's Lodge," Fall 2008

Effing Journal, "(or pigsty)" and "(draft)," Summer 2009

Eleven Eleven, "Last Song" and "Coda," Summer 2011

Esque, "Insufflation Feast," January 2011

Harvard Advocate, "The Sea Beyond This World" and "or Manhattan," Spring 2011

Lana Turner: A Journal of Poetry & Opinion, "(spectacle & pigsty)," Fall 2008

Tongue: A Journal of Writing & Art, "(nightly we are taken)," Fall 2011

Two Lines Online, Sections 6-9 of "On the Way to the Site of Doppo's Lodge," Summer 2011

Kiwao Nomura was born October 20, 1951 in Saitama Prefecture, Japan. He graduated from Waseda University, majoring in Japanese literature. A leading writer of the post-war generation, he is in the forefront of contemporary poetry. At the same time, he is known to be a prolific critic, translator, and essayist on comparative poetics. His work has been translated into many languages and published in magazines abroad, especially in France and the United States. He has performed internationally and released two CDs of collaborations with musicians. He played a leading role in the Contemporary Poetry Festival 95: Poetry Goes Out and the Contemporary Poetry Festival 97: Dance and Poésie. In 2007, he organized The Festival of International Poetry: Toward the Pacific Rim. From August to November 2005, he was a fellow at the International Writing Program at the University of Iowa in the United States. In December of the same year, he served as a director of the Japan-European Contemporary Poetry Festival in Tokyo."

Table of Contents

Introduction

Famous for electrifying performances of his work, Kiwao Nomura is revered in Japan, where he has been awarded major literary honors, including the Rekitei Prize for Young Poets and the prestigious Takami Jun Prize. His inspired work as a writer, editor, performer, organizer, and critic has altered the landscape of contemporary Japanese literature. Two CDs of his readings with musicians have generated a following in both Japan and France.

Nomura's work is iconoclastic—at once playful and heady, saturated by his interest in philosophy, Japanese shamanism, music and art. A poem ostensibly about a pigsty and Oedipal fixation incorporates references to Nietzsche and French philosopher Emmanuel Levinas in such a way as to suggest the pigsty as a metaphor for self and poem. (Nomura's insistent syntactical conjunction of "pigsty" and "I" underscores this metaphor). Throughout his work, Nomura overlays the visible world of criss-crossing streets with the microscopic world of "nerve ants," refusing to acknowledge any fundamental difference between cosmic and molecular, far and near, moment and whole, instant and eternity. His poetics, as such, run current with the writings of philosopher Gilles Deleuze, whose books (on cinema and on Nietzsche, in particular) stress the importance of intuition and insight as a means for disrupting our creatural habits. Both Deleuze and Nomura envision reality as ceaseless movement and invention.

The longest sequence included here is based on a pilgrimage to the place where Kunikida Doppo, a celebrated poet from the turn of the century, once lived. Stylistically, the poem takes place in what French theorist Guy Debord might call "Situationist Drift." Doppo's lodge site is real in as much as it is a historical marker of the spot where Doppo once lived, but it is not real, since the lodge collapsed long ago and the city of Tokyo has risen around its ruin. While the poem's speaker ambles through the city toward the lodge site in order to pay homage to the old poet, he remembers Doppo's poems and wrestles with the continuous, even "infinite" presence of the past in the obliterations and transformations of the present. As his meditation intensifies, he gradually releases himself from the impossible ambition of arriving at any meaning small enough to be nested in the toponym (as Nomura calls it) or *manifestation* (as Deleuze calls it), "Doppo's Lodge." Instead, the sojourning poet submits himself to chance encounters and perceptions, following the Deleuzian insight that "All becomes clear…if, beyond these manifestations, we aim our quest at Life itself." Along the way to the site of Doppo's lodge, a fabulous weave of recurring talismanic terms, wild shifts in tonal register, and word play keep both pilgrim-poet and reader alert and in thrall.

I

（そして豚小屋）

私は豚小屋が
ひとはひと星は星にうんざりして
いま異様に飴のように伸びてくる闇その闇かも

私は豚小屋が
その闇のなかをぽつぽつと光の染みさながらに
回帰する豚よあわれ

母の病んだ松果体の下の
私は豚小屋が
その永劫の梁から洩れる闇に溺れている叫び

私は豚小屋が
その叫びをなおも聴き取ろうとするとき
私より五倍も私なるべし

母の病んだ松果体の下の
私は豚小屋が
その永劫の梁に陽が糞尿のように激しく降る

あるいは糞尿が陽のように
私は豚小屋が
湯気を立てて笑う沈黙の土豊かならしむ

たがいに内に曲がり外に曲がり
たがいに促され誘惑されまたゆるやかに拘束され
私は豚小屋が

私は豚小屋が
眩暈とは全体が中心となることである
と知りコナラの葉むらひるがえるうつつ

毎日が眩暈だその縁から泡のように吹きこぼれて
私は豚小屋が
惑乱の私のかけらをさがす変かしら

(spectacle & pigsty)

it's pigsty I
the darkness maybe darkness stupendously stretching out now like taffy
man fed up with man star with star

it's pigsty I
pity the pig that eternally returns
to the darkness as spattering splotches of light

below Mother's diseased pineal gland
it's pigsty I
screaming drowning in a dark that fenestrates the eternal joist

it's pigsty I
must be five times more I than I
when trying to listen to the scream

below Mother's diseased pineal gland
it's pigsty I
gushing sunlight like nightsoil onto the eternal joist

or the nightsoil like sunlight
it's pigsty I
who mulch silence's muck while it laughs, steaming

each bent in bent out
each urged, cajoled, or shackled gently to another
it's pigsty I

it's pigsty I
vertigo: when the whole becomes center
attuned to the place where fat oak leaves flutter

every day is vertigo its margins boiling over like foam
it's pigsty I
eyeing pieces of I in bewilderment weird is it not?

私は豚小屋が
おお板々しい隙間から燃える頭蓋骨が見える
鹿色のオオスミハルカが流れ込んでくる

おお板々しい眠りの暑い壁
みつめているとぷつぷつと穴があき
私は豚小屋が

私は豚小屋が
なおも穴があき這い出てくる喃語の虫よ
私はやや肌に粟粒を生じをり

私は豚小屋が
死に給ひゆく母よ私を嚥下せよ嚥下せよ
そうして二度ともう私をひりだすな

二度ともう私をひりだすな母よ
私は豚小屋が
このむずがゆい身熱にすぎぬこのかたまりを

私は豚小屋が
いくつかの顔を浮かべてもみなまぼろし
その下から溶けた若い娘のような飢餓よあわれ

永遠が馬のかたちをして走り去ってゆくとき
私は豚小屋が
回帰してくるのは豚だいつも豚だ

私は豚小屋が
運んでいる不穏な筋肉隠れている
よい孤独わるい孤独朽ちかけの朽ちかけの

私は豚小屋が
ぬかるんでいる通路をどのように豚小屋へ
接続されるのかを知らず冬の夕ぐれ

it's pigsty I
see the burning skull through the pain-board gaps oh
fawn-colored Whirlaway gallops by

the thick fire wall of pain-board sleep oh
perforated with pinholes staring out
it's pigsty I

it's pigsty I
babbling bugs clamoring through the perforations
it's like I'm coming down with a rash of pinheads

it's pigsty I
swallow me swallow me Mother expiring
and never again shit me out

never shit me out again Mother
it's pigsty I
this crawling body this wad of nothing but heat

it's pigsty I
imagine faces but they're phantoms under
which the face of a girl comes clear as starvation

when eternity canters off in the shape of a horse
it's pigsty I
it's pig always pig that returns

it's pigsty I
packed with menacing muscles tensed
decent solitude crappy solitude crumbling crumbling

it's pigsty I
didn't notice in the winter dusk how
the muddy corridor leads to the pigsty

私は豚小屋が
この地上わけもなくコンビニに火をつけたくなり
筋肉がひかり豚小屋がうごめく

it's pigsty I
burning to set an earthly convenience store on fire no reason whatsoever
that muscles gleam and piggies wiggle

（そしてぼくはきみを抱いて）

そしてぼくはきみを抱いて　　ひと夏が締めくくられた
恵みの夜の郊外から　　また始まる都市の日常へと
車で帰路を急いでいたら　　丘の向こうで
花火の打ち上がるのがみえた

もしきみが助手席にいたら　　歓声をあげただろう
ぼくはハンドルをにぎっていたので　　愛する大地
愛する大地　　そこから届けられる火の花束を
視野の片隅に認めていただけ

でも十分だった　　今年の花火の向こうに
去年の花火がみえ　　そのまた向こうに
おととしの花火がみえていた

のにちがいなく　　空の奥で
いくつもの夏の終わりが連なって
夜の喉のようにすぼまり　　それが永遠

(and when I embraced you)

and when I embraced you   summer was over
from the suburbs of the gushing night   to the city the mundane resumed
rushing home in my car   over the hill
I saw a bottle rocket exploding

had you been close by in the passenger seat you'd have cried in delight
I was at the wheel so that as   my sweet old earth
my sweet old earth   the bouquet of flames was delivered
I tracked it only with the corner of my eye

although that was plenty   over this year's fireworks
I envisioned last year's   fireworks over
the fireworks of the year before that

I saw no doubt   in the depths of the sky
a chain of many summer's endings
tapering like night's throat   into eternity

ゆるやかな蝶番

いましきりと雨条のなかを
私は鳥がはばたいて消え去るのをみた
つまりしきりと
私ははばたいて鳥が消え去るのをみた
またはべつの呪文もあり
鳥が消え去るのをはばたいてみた私は
などと実りなく
鳥が私は消え去るのをはばたいてみた
あたりは静かでまるで静かで
はばたいて私は消え去るのをみた鳥が
狂念もうこれっきりと
はばたいてみた鳥が消え去るのを私は
抱きとめて
いや書きとめて
消え去るのをはばたいて私は鳥がみた
狂念もうこれっきりと
消え去るのを鳥がみた私ははばたいて
あたりは静かでまるで静かで
みた私は消え去るのを鳥がはばたいて
などと実りなく
みた鳥ははばたいて消え去るのを私が
またはべつの呪文もあり
鳥ははばたいてみた私が消え去るのを
つまりしきりと
鳥は私がはばたいて消え去るのをみた
いましきりと雨条のなかを

26

Barely Hinged

now in persistent strings of rain
I've seen a bird fluttering gone from sight
which is to say persistently
I've seen a fluttering bird gone from sight
so to speak in another incantation
seen I've gone from sight a bird fluttering
and so it goes in vain
seen a bird fluttering I've gone from sight
quiet around here it's completely quiet
a bird I've gone from sight seen fluttering
reverie enough
a bird gone from sight seen fluttering I've
embraced
or engraved
fluttering I've gone from sight seeing a bird
reverie enough
fluttering seen a bird gone from sight I've
gone quiet here it's completely quiet
gone from the sight fluttering I a bird seen
and so it goes in vain
gone from sight a bird seen I fluttering
so to speak in another incantation
a bird fluttering seen I've gone from sight
which is to say persistently
a bird I fluttering gone from sight seen
now in persistent strings of rain

散文考

そのとき私は
すべてを記憶した
記憶しなければならぬと思った

なぜそう思ったのかはよくわからないけれど
冬の夜だった
都心から西へ伸びる街道を
車でひたすらすすみ
危篤の母のもとへと急いでいた
ところが途中で工事渋滞に巻き込まれて
思わぬ時間を食ってしまった
ようやく渋滞を脱して
電波塔
先端に紫の照明灯を戴いて
それが妖しく夜空を彩る電波塔の下まで来たとき
不意に携帯が鳴り
私は車を路肩に停めて
母の臨終を伝える親族の声を聴いた
そのとき
大型のタンクローリーが
私の車の脇を通り抜けていったこと
街道の右の
煌煌と明るいコンビニエンスストアには
雑誌類を読む人がまばらにいて
蠅の頭のようにみえたこと
街道の左の
ゴルフ練習場はすでに閉まり
芝生に散らばるゴルフボールが
闇に浮かぶ水銀の粒か何かのようにみえたこと
それらすべてを私は記憶した
記憶しなければならぬと思った

それはいわば
私が臍帯の残滓を失って
決定的にこの世へと

On Prose

Then I
committed to memory everything
I felt compelled to remember

I don't know why I felt that way
but one winter night.
I was driving my car over the limits
along the highway that stretches west from Tokyo
hurrying to see my dying mother
but the traffic backed up
and I lost time
finally emerging from the congestion
a radio tower
crowned with radiant purple light
that eerily stained the night sky as I passed beneath it
my cell phone abruptly rang
I pulled over to the shoulder
and listened to a relative's voice tell me the hour of my mother's end
and then I noticed
that a large tanker truck
whooshed past within inches of my car
and that across the highway
inside the incandescently lit convenience store
a scattering of people were browsing magazines
and their heads looked like fly heads
and that on my side of the highway
inside the driving range already closed for the night
golf balls sprinkled on the grass
looked like mercury drops or something floating in the dark
I committed all of it to memory
compelled to remember

in other words
I lost at that moment the residue of my umbilical cord
and definitively tumbled into the world

いや宇宙へと放り出された瞬間なのだ
いわば私の
二度目の生誕の瞬間
そんな私を置き去りにするように
追い越してゆく冷凍車
つぎにスポーツカー
つぎにまた冷凍車
私はふと自分の古い詩句を思い出していた
錆と苔が行く
霊のぬけがけが行く
またオルガスムス屋が行く
フロントグリルから見上げれば
わずかながら空にまたたく星
そして何よりも電波塔
電波塔だった
その先端の
なぜかいちだんと明るさを増しながら
かっと私を見下ろしているような紫の照明灯
明日の安寧を不吉に
あるいは優しく明日の不穏を
告げているような照明灯
紫の異様に紫の
それを私は記憶した
記憶しなければならぬと思った

or rather into the universe
in other words it was
the moment of my second nativity
and as though it were leaving me behind
a refrigerated truck whooshed past me
followed by a sports car
followed by another truck
then some of my own verses occurred to me:
there goes rust and lichen
there goes the soul's departing shadow
there goes the orgasm peddler again
up through the windshield
a few stars sparkled in the sky
and above all the radio tower
the radio tower
from whose apex
purple illuminations glared fiercely down at me
in a kind of swelling intensity
as if the radiance
ominously announced the calm of tomorrow
or tenderly announced the unrest of tomorrow
the purple singularly purple
thing I committed to memory
I felt compelled to remember

ラストソング

キリンの赤ちゃんは
２メートルもの高さのお母さんから産み落とされるため
怪我することも多いという
キリンにかぎらない
生まれるとは
何かしら出会い頭の事故のようなものだ

存在の鳥肌
存在の鳥肌

ぼくもそうだった
泣きわめいているとお母さんがやってきて
ミルクとことばを与えられた
どちらもぬるっとするので吐き出す
するとお母さんは
学校というところにぼくを連れて行ってくれた

存在の鳥肌
存在の鳥肌

やがて股間が重たく感じられるようになったので
保健室に行って
女医の香織先生にみてもらうと
ぼくの股間にぼくと同じ無数の微細な人間たちがいて
はちきれんばかりなのだという

存在の鳥肌
存在の鳥肌

ぼくはまた泣いた
でももうお母さんは来てくれない
ぼくはひとりでぼくのなかの無数の人間たちとたたかった
たたかっているうちに
いつのまにか年老いてしまったらしい
ぼくのなかの人間たちはだいぶ減ったが

Last Song

Dropped two meters
from their mothers, giraffe babies
often hurt themselves they say
the giraffe's not an exception
birth is something akin
to a surprise smash

horripilation of being
horripilation of being

such was my own case
while I was wailing Mother showed up
and plied me with milk and words
both so gooey I spewed them out
then Mother
took me to that place called School

horripilation of being
horripilation of being

soon my groin took on weight
so I visited the school's sick room
and showed it to Lady Doctor Kaori
my groin is filled with innumerable minute humans identical to myself
and they're ready to burst out she said

horripilation of being
horripilation of being

I wailed some more
but Mother never returned
alone I battled the innumerable humans within me
and in that battle
I aged before I knew it
the population of those inner humans declined

われとわが身を眺めて
手指足指合わせて 20 本もあるということは
まだ常軌を逸しているような気がして
ばらまきたくなった

存在の鳥肌
存在の鳥肌

いまは秋
空気はおだやかに澄んで
ぼくという泣き虫をまるく包もうとしている
とりどりの黄や赤の葉っぱをそえて
人生は永遠よりも一日だけ短い
そんな気もしてくる
そのときだ
裏山ほどもあるひとりの大きな子供が
私を包む小さなまるい秋に気づき
サッカーボールのようにそれを蹴り上げようと
近づいてくる

存在の鳥肌
存在の鳥肌

but when I look at myself and my body
and fingers and toes twenty altogether
which seems really bizarre
I feel like scattering my seed

horripilation of being
horripilation of being

now it's autumn
the air calm and clear
roundly embracing the crybaby I am
with little leaves tinged yellow and red
life lasts forever and a day short
that's how I start to feel
at the very moment
a child as big as the backyard hill
spots the small round autumn embracing me
and he lumbers over
to kick it like a football

horripilation of being
horripilation of being

(あるいは顔貌)

（なぜか葡萄でした）

なぜか葡萄でした、
そのつやつやと輝く果皮に、
顔が映って、
プファの顔、
プフィの顔、
つぎつぎ、直立した手弱女の乳房のうえ、
乳房のわき、ころがり、
落ちてゆきました、

ヘンデルのメサイアの、
清らかな声、
流れていました、
顔たちも涙を浮かべ、
その涙にまた、別の顔が映って、

やがて、妣の国への、
サヨナラサヨナラサヨナラ、
という名の洞、
のなか、つぎつぎ、
送り込まれて、
プフィの顔、
プファの顔、
泣きながら、歪みながら、
押し込むのも顔、
押し込まれるのも顔、
最後には涙、果肉とぐちゃぐちゃにまざって、
なぜか葡萄でした、

（木に顔が咲いて）

木に顔が咲いて、
どこかここは、
木に顔が咲いて、

(or visage)

(They were grapes somehow)

they were grapes somehow,
the brilliant sheen on their skins,
reflected faces,
phew faces,
whew faces,
one after another, from the peaks of the sylph's uplifted breasts,
and rolling, past the tips of her breasts,
they tumbled down,

the serene chorus,
of Händel's *Messiah,*
continued,
tears welled on the faces,
reflecting more faces in tears,

rolling on, before long, to the land of dead mothers,
through the hollow named,
farewellfarewellfarewell,
sent off,
one after another,
phew faces,
whew faces,
wailing, grimacing,
some faces pushing in,
some faces pushed in,
at the end, tears and flesh mashed to a pulp,
they were grapes somehow,

(Faces blossom in the tree)

faces blossom in the tree,
where *here* is,
faces blossom in the tree,

たくさんの顔、私をみて、
私、うつむいて、穴だらけになって、
でも、剥くんだ、ひっそりと、
うなじのあたりから、
顔のない熱情、
いつかきっと、
顔のない熱情、

（生きるとは）

生きるとは、
濃密な闇、そのところどころ、
地から光が漏れて、
なんだろう、近づくと、
窓、地に穿たれた小さな窓、
開けると顔があらわれ、むくんだ顔、
打ちひしがれた顔があらわれ、
あわててその場を離れる、
つぎの窓を開ける、
今度は声だけ、たぶん録音された「主ヨ、
私ハ近ヅイテイマス」とか、
でもノイズが混じってよく聞こえない、
その場も離れ、生きるとは、
ようやく何番目かの窓で、一枚の、
地図のような顔、私の顔、
半ば泥に覆われて、
生きるとは、なお痙攣が、
繊い虫のように、
そこから逃れ出る、

many faces, eyeing me,
slumped, full of holes,
yet, I'm peeling, quietly,
from the nape,
ardor without a face,
someday I'll wish for,
ardor without a face,

(Life is)

life is,
clenched darkness, dotted,
with light blinking up through the ground,
I draw near, wondering what it is,
a window, drilled into the ground, a small window,
in which, as it opens, faces materialize, puffy faces,
grieving faces materialize,
I bolt away,
I open the next window,
this time just a voice, perhaps a prerecorded *Nearer,
My God, to Thee,* something like that
but drowned by background noises,
I leave that spot too, life is,
at long last, after several windows, a sheet of,
map-like faces, my face,
half-smeared with mud,
life is, in spasms,
squirming away from there,
like nightcrawlers,

デジャヴュ街道

デジャヴュ、
さながらてのひらのうえを走るように、
紙葉一枚ほどのくすんだ空の奥の、その右上あたりから、
道がひとすじ、濃くうすくあらわれ、
ちらめく蛇体のようにうねりながら、
私たちの眼のはるか下へ、たとえば立ったまま眠る
祖の腰のあたりへと伸びて——

オルガスムス屋が行く、
神経の蟻が行く、

と、その道をよぎるべつの道たちが、
デジャヴュ、
長短さまざまにちぎれた糸屑のさまをなして浮かび上がり、
まれには、少女の脛のうえの
かすれた傷痕のような風情をみせながら、
どれも一様に陽に照らされて、
右へ左へと揺れひかるので——

神経の蟻が行く、
錆と苔が行く、

こうして全体が
まるで地のおもてのどこかしらの、
デジャヴュ、
数知れぬ交叉路を身にまとった街道そのままに、
空のおもての鏡にでも映し出された、というように——

錆と苔が行く、
またオルガスムス屋が行く、

そうなのだ、
さらにつぶさに眺めると、
街道のところどころがわずかに捩れていて、だからその、
いわば脇腹や背の部分までもがいっときあらわにされ、

Déjà vu Avenue

déjà vu,
as though across the palm of the hand,
from the depths of the sky, opaque as a leaf of paper, from the upper
    right corner,
vividly, vaguely, a string of road appears,
serpentining, flickering,
far beyond the reach of our eyes, stretching toward
the lower back of our progenitor who, for example, sleeps standing up—

orgasm-monger plods past,
nerve-ants plod past,

and then, other roads crisscross this road,
déjà vu,
they show up like shredded yarn of different lengths,
suggesting something like a hazy scar,
barely there on a girl's knee,
every particle equally lit,
a shine that flashes right, then left—

nerve-ants plod past,
rust and moss plod past,

so as though the entire body
were reflected in the mirror of the sky's face,
like the avenue swathed in innumerable cross streets,
déjà vu,
somewhere on the face of the earth—

rust and moss plod past,
orgasm-monger plods past again,

it's certainly true,
upon further exhaustive examination,
the avenue twists here and there, and in doing so,

デジャヴュ、
ためになお一層、いのちとしての街道の、
息づき脈うっているのが際立たせられ——

オルガスムス屋が行く、
霊の抜けがけが行く、

かたわらには、
とりわけ脇道との付け根のあたりには、
水滴のようにこびりついた廃屋の数かぎりなく、
あるいは伸び放題の灌木の茂み、
干からびた犬の死骸らしきものも散見されて、
してみれば棄村の形跡はあきらかなのに、なぜ、なぜ
道だけが無疵のまま生々しく、
デジャヴュ、
空のおもてを縫ってなおもうねってゆくのか、
謎めいてゆくのか——

霊の抜けがけが行く、
また神経の蟻が行く、

おお、いったい何のための、
誰のための、これは通い路、
と問いかけたそのときだった、まさにそのとき、
空の奥のその街道のうえを、
ひとの痕跡を運び、
また食らう微細な生き物の列らしき影が、
さながらひとの染色体のように
ひとしきり激しく昇り降りするのを、
なすすべもなく私たちは眼に、
デジャヴュ、
したのだった——

神経の蟻が行く、
また錆と苔が行く、

その昇降管のなかを、その昇降管のなかを——

its so-called flank and spine are, for a moment, exposed,
déjà vu,
and furthermore, this confirms the avenue as a life form,
breathing and pulsing—

orgasm-monger plods past,
shedding-soul plies its plod,

away from the center,
nested especially in the crooks of byways,
the innumerable hulks of vacant houses cling like waterdrops,
and in the wild shrubs,
a scattering of something like the corpses of dogs,
makes evident the traces of a deserted village, yet how, how
can the road remain unscathed, exuberant,
déjà vu,
sutured to the face of the sky, vermiculating
into enigma—

shedding-soul plies its plod,
again nerve ants plod past,

oh, for what possible reason
or for whom was this passage made,
and at the precise instant when that question was posed, at that very moment,
on the avenue piercing the sky's depths,
we witnessed, helplessly,
a column of shadows of microscopic creatures
transporting and feeding on human remains,
déjà vu,
as they fiercely marched,
for a few intense moments,
as though they were human chromosomes—

nerve-ants plod past,
again rust and moss plod past,

up and down through the tube, up and down through the tube—

（雨）

名づけるとは
むかし**雨**という
柔らかな女神の行列がそうしたように
寺院や魚や
大地や草を
はこべやははこぐさを
うっすらと濡らすこと
乾いてきたら
また名づけ直さなければならない
われわれというありかたが
雨なのだ
投げ網のように柔らかく降りかかる
雨

(rain)

to name
(as a soft procession of goddesses
called **rain**
once did)
by wetting
temples and fish
earth and grass
chickweed and cudweed
when they go dry
we must rename them
rain is
our mode of existence
rain
softly falling like a fine net

二

II.

（あるいは波）

わたくしの果ての世の月明かりの
液晶の海に
ちらちら
みえているのは
あれは人魚でも波でもなく
眠れない女たち

人のうち
どこまでもやわらかく
重たげな肉をうねらせ分泌にみち
眠れない
とりわけ眠れない女たち

おおたえまなく寝返りをうつ女たち眠れない眠れない
するとたとえようもなく
うなじの明るみ
針を刺すと
ぞろぞろと白い虫たちがあふれ出すような

その照り映え
その照り映え
その照り映え

捕獲の網を手に
誰だわたくしは
夏の日の少年でもあるまいし
ただこんなにも睾丸が

48

(or waves)

La mer de la veillée, telle que les seins d'Amélie.
—Arthur Rimbaud

What you see in the sea,
those aren't mermaids.
What you see in the sea,
those are only waves.

—Nakahara Chûya

at the edge of the world within me
illuminated by moonlight
flickering
in a liquid crystal sea
are neither mermaids nor waves
but sleepless women

more than anything else
thoroughly soft
rolling heavy flesh weeping secretions
sleepless women
more than anything else sleepless

oh turning incessantly and tossing the women sleepless sleepless
and beyond words
the luminescence of their necks
if pricked by a pin
would unleash pale squirming worms

such glittering
such glittering
such glittering

with a butterfly net in hand
who am I
not some boy in the summer afternoon
although my balls

49

睾丸だけが
卵黄のように垂れた月をまねて重い

そのあいだにも
眠れない女たちのすさまじいパーティだパーティ
ひとりが
パンプスをはいたままベッドを飛び越え
蹴り上げる昼の鬱屈の隣で
べつのひとりが
ベッドをたてて
くるくるとまわし始める
ワルツもうどうしようもなくワルツその照り映えその照り映え

わたくしの果ての世の月明かりの
液晶の海に
ちらちら
みえているのは
あれは人魚でも波でもなく
眠れない女たち

my balls incredibly are heavy
as the moon drooping like an egg yolk

meanwhile
the spectacular party yes the party of sleepless women goes on
one
in stilettos leaps over a bed
clicking her heels at the atrabilious day
and another
lifts the mattress on its side
and spins it
to the waltz the ceaseless waltz such glittering such glittering

at the edge of the world within me
illuminated by moonlight
flickering
in a liquid crystal sea
are neither mermaids nor waves
but sleepless women

この世の彼方の海

この世の彼方の海（なんて
あったらいいね（ふと（ふわっと
思いついたんだけど（想像力は死んだ
想像せよ（と古来言われてきたレベルで（みたいに
この世とは襞のこと
彼方とはまた襞のこと（襞の襞の
しなやかな打ち返し（を超え（う、うみ
なんてね（でもさ
イメージしてしまう癖（あるある
それはたぶん
宇宙の闇のどこかに浮いてるんだ（浮いてる？
海が？（そう（ふわっと
水の胎のとおい成り立ち（ちがう
さわさわと（ひっかき跡のような
たくさんの線の（わずかの緑の（静かの海の
柔らかい岩石のように浮いて（みたいに
あまりそのことを考えると
主体が（つまりきみの頭が（ってこと
砕かれてしまう（なんてね（う、うみ
ふと（思いついたんだけど
波の飛沫ぐらい（あるある
浴びていたいよ

この世の彼方の海（と（長いあいだ
ふつうの海と（さんざん（脳髄のなかを泳ぎまわってきた
しじま（ふわっと（どこがどう
どこがどうちがうのでしょう
そのしじま（ふと（ふつうの海は
うねります（水母のように
この世の彼方の海（は（ふるえて漂い出し
ねり歩きます（ここは（舌の泥濘
ふつうの海（は（月と親しく
ねぶりねぶられ（この（舌の
世の彼方の（ばかあかい（海は（ばかあかい
それ自体が月（のよう（泥濘

52

The Sea Beyond This World

a sea beyond this world (what if
there was (just a (fuzz
of thought I had (imagination's dead
imagine (we're told for untold ages to imagine
the meaning of the world as folds
and the beyond as folds
over the elastic roll (of fold on fold (sss... sea
(like that (still
we imagine out of habit (yes-yes
perhaps
somewhere in the dark universe floating (floating?
a sea? (yes (fuzzy
distant source, a watery uterus (no
babbling (like abrasions
profuse grooves (a speck of green
in the sea of tranquility (floating like soft rock (as
if you consider it too much
the subject (which is your head (so to speak
would crash down (like that (sss...sea
just (a thought but
it's the spray at least (yes-yes
in which I would be soaked

the sea beyond this world (and (for a long time
the ordinary sea (again, again (having swum in the encephaloid
quietude (fuzz (in what way
in what way are they different
in that quietude (just the (ordinary sea
swells (like a medusa
the sea beyond this world (palpitating (adrift
promenading (this one as (a glossal mire
the ordinary sea (so (moon-inclined
tonguing and tongued (this (tongue
beyond all world (sinister red (the sea (sinister red
itself like (a moon (a mire

だからさ
この世の彼方の海（なんて（つねにすでに
あったかもね（ひとびとはそこへ
思い思いに舟を曳いた（ぼくも運び入れよう
キス（手紙（あす抱く
きみの肉の惑わしのエキス
なんてね（すべてを運び入れたら
もうすることがない（舟はほそまり（千の線となり
ダイヤグラムまぶしい（みたいに
そのたくさんの線のうえでなら
ぼくは生きられる（ってこと（想像せよ
ぼくの（表皮のいたみも
きみにそそぎ（そこねた精液の（ほろほろしたしずくも
線（なのだ
死のときのノイズ（も

and you see
the sea beyond this world (so to speak (already and always
took place (people there
tugged their boats where they pleased (and I'll breach
kiss (address (tomorrow embrace
the winsome distillate of your flesh
so to speak (when everything is breached
there's nothing left to do (boats move (as a thousand grooves
dazzling diagrams
and only on those grooves
can I survive (imagine (that
the stinging surface (of my skin and
beaded tears of (semen that never (poured into you
are (grooves
as well (as the sounds at our death

（あるいはマンハッタン）

マンハッタンとは
そこに近づくということだ

ＪＦＫ空港からイエローキャブに乗って
私たちは目を凝らしつづけた
なかなかみえてこないね
と妻はいう（はじめてモロッコに
砂漠をみに行ったときもそうだったじゃないか
と私はなぐさめる

近づくことがすべて
マンハッタンとは
ひとつの砂漠（であるのかもしれない

そしてようやく
遠く蜃気楼のように
スカイスクレーパー群のシルエットが浮かび上がってきた
私たちは少し興奮し（ナツメヤシの茂るオアシスの町エルフードから
ランドローバーで三十キロ（いちめんの
土と岩の広がりの向こうに
たおやかな（あまりにもたおやかな
黄金色の砂丘のうねりが見えてきたとき（私たちは
少し興奮し

マンハッタンとは
自然の驚異そのもの（であるのかもしれない

それは近くの（クイーンズ？
ブルックリン？　建物や看板に隠れて
すぐにみえなくなってしまう（みえなくなって
またあらわれる（そのあいだに
成長し大きくなる
近づくという悦び
近づくという苦しみ

(or Manhattan)

Manhattan is
to approach Manhattan

taking a yellow cab from JFK and
still looking for it
when I wonder will it show up
asks my wife (same case
when we went to see the Moroccan desert wasn't it
I calm her down

it's all about the approach
Manhattan is
its own desert (perhaps

and finally
like a distant mirage
the silhouette of that throng of skyscrapers comes clear
we are thrilled a little (from the oasis town of Erfoud lush with date palms
thirty kilometers by Land Rover (beyond
the tracts of dirt and rocks
graceful (so exquisitely graceful
golden swells of dunes rising (we
were thrilled a little

Manhattan is
nothing but a marvel of nature (perhaps

behind the neighboring (Queens?
Brooklyn? buildings and billboards it slinks
off and disappears (disappears
and reappears (meanwhile
growing more intense
the pleasures of approach
the anguish of approach

その交錯のあいだに（マンハッタンとは
成長し大きくなる

だがそのとき
それをふたたび隔てるように
高架地下鉄の赤錆びた橋梁（ほんとうに鮮やかに赤錆びて（だから
それを透かしてスカイスクレーパー群
その対比がまるでアメリカの光と影そのもののように

あるいは（こうもいえるだろう
マンハッタンが私たちへの贈り物であるとするなら
赤錆びた橋梁は
それをやや冗談のきついリボンのように飾って
私たちに差し出す（あるいは

マンハッタンとは
狂暴（であるのかもしれず
それをへだてる赤錆びた優しい檻
檻が縦や斜めに（唐草模様のように交錯して
私たちの頬を染める

けれどもさらに
その交錯を剥きあらわれ（かぎりなく
剥きあらわれ（剥きあらわれ（剥きあらわれ
もうリボンもなく頬もなく
林立の
無人の喉のように

マンハッタンとは
剥きあらわれ（剥きあらわれ

気がつくと
もうクイーンズボロ橋を渡りきって
私たちはまだ
無人の喉への
挨拶の言葉をもたない

in a mesh (Manhattan is
growing more intense

and then
as though to shield it again
an elevated subway's rusty viaduct (rusty in pure bright auburn (behind
which the throng of skyscrapers
stand in contrast like the light and shade of America herself

or (let's put it this way
if Manhattan were a gift for us
it's been decorated with rusty viaduct
like a ribbon of crude joke
and thrust at us (or

Manhattan is
pure ferocity (perhaps
its gentle cage of rusty auburn shields it
the cage vertically and diagonally (meshed like arabesque patterns
ruddling our cheeks

and yet
the mesh unbinds and the city emerges (endlessly
unbinds and (unbinds and (unbinds and it emerges
the ribbon and cheeks left
circumvented by a forest
of throated hollows

Manhattan is
unbinding and emerging (unbinding and emerging

suddenly
having crossed the Queensboro Bridge
we pull up short
of a greeting
to those throated hollows

（ある日、突然）

ある日、突然、
何もすることがなく、
なって、空蝉、からから、
夏あみ、だぶつ、
ああいっそ、
妊婦とセックス、して、
みたい、ぼくは、すてきだろうなあ、
まるく膨らんだ、スイカのような、
おなか、ちたちた、舌で、
登ったり、駆け下りたり、
妊婦の、
魔の、山の、
妊娠線、恐そう、稲妻みたい、
なぞったり、それたり
胎児の心音、聴いたり、
あ、動いた、なんて、
愛する大地、
愛する大地、
遊んでいるうちに、ごはんですよ、
じゃなかった、山の、ふもとの、
毛の、絶対繁茂する、
世界のみなもと、
から呼ばれて、すてきだろうなあ、
ぼくは、ペニスを入れて、
胎児の、すぐそばに、
マイクみたいに近づけて、近づけて、
そっと、採集、するんだ、
「超人」の、
「星の子供」の、
大きすぎる頭から洩れる、
親殺しのささめきを。

(one day, suddenly)

One day, suddenly,
I have nothing,
left to do, life, empty shell, rattles,
summer netted up, bucket kicked, Amitabha Buddha,
ah, rashly,
I wouldn't mind, making love to,
a pregnant woman, how sweet it would be,
over that swollen, protuberant belly, like a watermelon,
my tongue, flicking,
sliding, up and down,
her Magic,
Mountain,
along the stretch mark, unnerving, like a lightning bolt,
tracing it, and divagating,
and listening, to the fetus's cardiacal whoosh-whoosh,
like, *oh, it just moved,*
my sweet old earth,
my sweet old earth,
while I'm fooling around, *it's dinnertime,*
well not really, though, I am being called,
to the base of that mountain,
where hair, absolutely luxuriates,
to be called, how splendid,
I would, insert my penis,
nearer and nearer,
to the fetus, like a microphone,
delicately, to catch,
escaping from the outsized head,
of "the overman,"
of "the star child,"
its parricidal whisper.

会陰讃

1
誰?　筋組織はよく発達している
行為のためにマニュアルをもつことは不便だと思う
え?　誰?　恥が表面から表面へと
終わることなく跳ね返る
ひだが下にずうっと連なっている
えっ?　誰?　キメ検知される
すべてがつねにいくぶんか間違いである
境界の消え方やあらわれ方が多重の光のようだ
えっ?　会陰?　ひろがるちぢれた波
時の向こう側が少しだけめくれている
誰?　会陰?
誰?　会陰?

2
詩人が会陰について書くのは
おそらく私がはじめてだろう
ぎうぎうぎう
遠隔のきみを孕ませながら
みずからを会陰たらしめたいと思う

3
会陰のうえに立つと不思議だ
(と神経の蟻は語る)
古い裂開の記憶がさわさわとひろがり
ついで縫合の未来が
つる草のように音もなく上書きされてゆく
隣では
性愛の
ぬぷたふぬぷたふ
なんとひらがなに満ちていることか

4
母の母の
そのまた母の

Panegyric to the Perineum

1.
who is it? its muscular tissue supple
but so inconvenient to come to the act with a manual
what? who? all the intimate way across
endlessly elastic
folding into its own depths
what? who? sheathed in silkiness
everything usually something of an accident
the edge coming and going like bands in a spectrum
what? the perineum? ripples spread outward
and time's nether side is slightly evaginated
who? the perineum?
who? the perineum?

2.
perhaps I'm the first
poet to write about the perineum
shovingstuffingit
in the distance impregnating you
I'm lusting to perineumize myself

3.
strange to balance on the perineum
(observes a nerve-ant)
the susurrous memory of an old laceration spreads
instigating a suture in the future
that silent as a vine overwrites the memory
across the squishsquash
of an onomatopoetic
erotics

4.
our mother's mother's
and her own mother's
and it seems we were searching, no?,

滋味あふれる陥没の跡
それを探し歩いていたらしいのね私たち
（と別の神経の蟻は語る）
途中で道を何度も間違えて辿り直したり
探索の場のなんというプラトー
あるいは会陰
はるか崖下に松林が異様に青く広がり
その青さに見覚えがあると思ったのね私たち
会陰を降りてゆく

5
もう会陰しかない
どこからか血が噴きこぼれてきて
生きて薄い脇レベルもう会陰しか
ない（笑い）身がらは左側に逸れて捩れ
右側や向こう側が入り乱れて滲みてくる
夢の表ではダチョウのように痩せた老詩人が
声の薄明をしきりに織り上げもう会陰
しかないわたくしは女つぶやかれてしまう
またたくまの廃墟またたく股（笑い）の廃墟
やや遠い薄膜のように心を思い描きもう
会陰しかない眼の奥が絞られるほど眩しくて
言葉の裏に住むざわめきの虫もわたくしは女（笑い）
誘い出されてしまう死後にもリズムは在れ
離接したらまた人知れず裂開のあふれて
遅れて骨のきりもなく届く藻のように
マドンナのまわりをまわるスペルマプフィよ
スペルマプファよもう会陰しかない
円周率さえ歌い出して砥骨（笑い）にも
仙骨（笑い）にも雷が発生して
もう会陰しかない

64

for that fertile recess
(suggests another nerve ant)
we now and then go off track and retrace
the nexus of our intention that mound
or the perineum
down below the bluff the pine grove singularly blue
and imagine we've seen that blue before
going down the banks of the perineum

5.
nothing but the perineum
and from somewhere the gush of blood
arrives, alive, nothing but the
perineum (laughter) the subject thrashes and twists to the left
so the right and the other side emerge from the turmoil
in the dream a poet straggly as an ostrich
orchestrates the shimmering voices nothing but
the perineum I a woman it whispers
ruined in the wink of an eye ruined in the wink between thighs
(laughter)
like the deep membrane an imagination of the heart
nothing but the perineum so dazzling I squint behind my eye
behind words buzzing like insects I too am a woman (laughter)
it lures me out the rhythm throbbing posthumously
then breaking secretly overbrimming itself
until at last boneless as algae
and circling that Madonna dear spermata-zoe
dear spermata-zed and nothing but the perineum
bursting into a song of pi as thunder blooms on the stapes (laughter)
and the sacrum (laughter)
nothing but the perineum

息吹節

這う眼のさきへ息。
こころみに吹きかけて。
息のした。たまらなく秘匿され。
たまらなく胚かなにか。
ニュートリノ。
燐光は立ち。
めぐりはいまも生まれたてのへこみや突起のうえ。
たまらなく渚。パレード。
水を通さない実名詞のうす膜。
それ。おまえはそれ。
たまらなくあえぎハアハアと。
たまらなくあやうく。
ひくく。
さらに水よりもひくく。
這う眼のさきへ息。
うちふるえ。なりあわさり。なりあまり。
こころみにヒトデ。
こころみに藻。
女波。
もの狂いの額ほどにあらわれている海！
呼ぶと呼ばれて。
走りだすひとのあぶら身あわく。
なまの。たまらなくなまの。
いつわりの。
まだ影を含む。
まだ泡。まだ水母のまなざし。
まだ羊腸をまねている傷痕。
からみあい。ねじれ。のぼってゆき。
さける。
さけぶ。
そぼ濡れの卑語らひらき。
流木ら。
へい。ペニンスラ！
何かしら手斧。
こころみに蛸へのドア。

Insufflation Feast

a breath ahead of the eyes crawling.
tentatively exhaled.
underblown. unbearably obscured.
unbearably embryo or some such.
a neutrino.
phosphorescing.
still flowing across fresh pits and nubs.
unbearably promontory. a parade.
a watertight membrane of actual nouns.
one. you're the one.
unbearably sucking air rasping and gasping.
unbearably precarious.
lower.
lower than water.
a breath ahead of the eyes crawling.
quavering. growing harmonic. going superfluous.
tentatively starfish.
tentatively algae.
a woman wave.
the sea revealing its lunatic forehead!
called in the act of calling.
the starting runner's fatty tissue diminishes.
bare. unbearably bare.
feigned.
still containing its own shadow.
still foams. still the gaze of sea nettles.
still the scar twisting anguine.
tangled. convolute. climbing.
tearing open.
shrieking.
sopping with vulgarisms.
driftwood.
give me. headlands!
somehow an adz.
tentatively a door to an octopus.

たまらなく無名骨の蠱惑。
静謐。
空。どこへでも垂れて。
その大きな指のはらによっても消しえないよ。
たまらなく脈。
粒子状ざらざら。
それ。おまえはそれ。
這う眼のさきへ息。
息のした。夢のした。
思いのほか刺青めくそのけざやかめ。
たまらなくめくられ。
たまらなくむきだしの。
純粋の。
それ。ダンサーのあえなさ。
サムライのうすぺらさ。
縁日のふかさ。
そしてようやく頑ぜないセックス。
ようやく圭角をそがれた神経。
呑む。うたう。出かけてゆく。
かまうな。
息は送りかえされない。
たまらなく波瀾にとみ。
たまらなく謎めいて。
たまらなく風。
こころみに耳。
いまここに胎蔵されるべき。
それ。息のかたち。
こころみられて。
みえる曠野の不充足のさき。
ごった煮の道々をぬけて手にない蛇のうねる聖痕よ。

unbearaby seduced by the innominate bone.
tranquility.
the sky. sagging anywhere at all.
nor rubbed out by the bulb of the big thumb.
unbearably pulses.
particularly gritty.
the one. you're the one.
a breath ahead of the eyes crawling.
underblown. an underblown dream.
the tattooed lotus turns turtle.
unbearably unveiled.
unbearably bare.
pure.
the one. transient as a dancer.
flimsy as a samurai.
shrine day's depths.
and finally unguardedly making love.
finally filing down the nerve ends.
to swallow. to sing. to go out.
never mind.
the breath never returns.
unbearably tumultuous.
unbearably enigmatic.
unbearably breeze.
tentatively ear.
retained in utero here and now.
the one. breathshape.
tried out.
looking past the flatland's insufficiency.
and the hodgepodge paths to the serpent-slithering stigmata of an
    empty hand.

（私たち、芥をちりばめて狂い……）

私たち、芥をちりばめて狂い、
芥を
ちりばめて狂い、

——おお空の息口

春めき、ふぞろいな、
空の息口、ふぞろいな、
この土地の不思議なひだ、
不老川、
自生するままにそこに、私たち、芥をちりばめて狂い、

—— 藁の女神は春スキー、

風が立ち働く、
記憶の輪がふわっとふくれる、

——藁の女神は春スキー、

だがとりわけ、ひだ、不思議なひだ、
シャワーの快感にとりこめられた生活の小丘よりも、
みよ、縄のようによじれ
ほどかれてゆくひだ、
不老川、

——そこに蛇もひそみ、妖星も落ち、

そして私たちもまた
眼をとじれば灼かれ、ちいさな骨となり、
ひとの膣で哭くまでの変態、
おおそのように、
灰であり、灰のみえない運び手、

——そこに蛇もひそみ、妖星も落ち、

(scattering dust, we go crazy...)

scattering dust, we go crazy,
dust,
go scattering crazy,

—oh, the sky's breathmouth,

springlike, erratic,
the sky's breathmouth, erratic,
curious folds of landscape,
Stillflow River,
running feral there, we go crazy, scattering dust,

—the straw goddess goes spring skiing,

wind diligently at work,
circling fluff of reminiscence,

—the straw goddess goes spring skiing,

and above all, the folds, the curious folds,
over quotidian hills pent up in a pleasure of showers,
lo, and kinked like rope,
then the folds are drawn out,
Stillflow River,

—where a snake skulks, and a meteor plunges,

as we are,
when we close our eyes, ablaze, nothing but small bones,
metamorphogenic then wailing in a stranger's vagina,
oh, like that, we are,
ashes, invisibly bearing ashes,

—where a snake skulks, and a meteor plunges,

このくるめきの奥はふかく、涼しく、
最後に
むなしさが輝度を得る。

the core of this crazedness cool, and deep,
until
the void goes purely radiant.

三

III.

独歩住居跡のほうへ

明確な碑を避けること……
　　　　　　──ヴィクトール・セガレン

1　（序）

独歩住居跡のほうへ、
住居跡
独歩
のほうへ──

（その瞬間、滑りこむようにあらわれ、
組みあわさる光芒──

それは
空白という名の空白をめぐるように、
それはまた
空白が空白を越えながらなお空白にとどまるように、
のがれゆく地と
地をのがれゆく断片、

（しかしまた、眠る蝶のような、
畳まれた、隠しつくされた──

住居
跡
のほうへ、──国、木、田、
微細、（ゲームの
轟音はるか）、
めくるめくまでに。

On the Way to the Site of Doppo's Lodge

To avoid any definitive stele
—Victor Segalen

1 (prelude)

On the way to the site of Doppo's lodge,
lodge
site
toward, Doppo,—

(when suddenly, beams of light
bend into sight and interlace—

as if
circling the vacancy called vacancy,
or as if
vacancy while staying vacancy transcends vacancy,
averting earth and
earth-averting shards,

(and yet, like a sleeping butterfly,
folded, and hidden away—

on the way to
the lodge
site— *kuni* 国 land, *ki* 木 tree, *da* 田 field,
the infinitesimal, (roar of
a distant game),
kaleidoscope.

2（不意に道はひらかれた）

きわめて揺れて
不意に道はひらかれた
石の飢えひくく微細街区のわずかな土くれのうえ
日の泡の
畝また畝もまぼろし
空域にはやる足裏の炎は手なづけ
反復彷徨の
独歩住居跡よ。

墓碑パルコの縁辺に薄日さすことのまれまれ
憩う間際に
ゆらめきすすむ何の軌跡なら辿りえようか
ここまでの恍惚ここで別れよう
ここに雪片は舞い
不安裂開の
独歩住居跡よ。

微風そのうらに名の剥落は尽き
三度や九度の
仮死の卵のあしらいにも半睡をひいて耐えた
誰の脳の中にもない外にもない
問いの巣の住居跡
独歩しずかに。

光芒またも組みあわさるだろう動不動の泥のへりへそ
そのへりのないへそにこそ
文字の初期は震えまたたき
問いの巣の住居跡
独歩しずかに。

2 (a path abruptly opens)

With an eruptive tremor
a path abruptly opens
onto hungry stones in dirt between infinitesimal city blocks
the mundane froth
ridge after ridge of illusion
pervades the puff of airspace from my hard-pressed heel
in the recurrent drift
at the site of Doppo's lodge.

How curiously pale rays limn the Tombstone Emporium?
edged with stillness
how to locate a trace in the flickering
here we'll say goodbye to ecstasy so far
in a dance of anxiety-dehiscing
snowflakes at
the site of Doppo's lodge.

Names exfoliate in a back-eddy of breeze
for a time and times
with its asphyxiated egg inside, the nest survives active indifference,
    abeyant
not inside not outside of nobody's brain
the lodge site as a nest of questions,
Doppo's quiet *pas seul.*

Lightbeams will interlace again over the mud's shifting, shiftless edge
    and depth
over its very edgeless depths
an incunabula of ideograms quivers and flickers
the lodge site as a nest of questions
Doppo's quiet *pas seul.*

3（半自由に）

（あ、たんにひとつの杭）
そのような叫びがかつて指さしていた空域
その空域にいまも私は
独歩住居跡
とひたすら読む
（石の飢えひくく微細街区のわずかな土くれのうえ）

つまりまだビルとかが建つまえの、サラ地、というのだったか、むきだ
しになった土くれの粒子ひとつひとつが、冬の陽を浴びていわば励
起しているかのような、渋谷は墳墓パルコの縁辺あたりであったろう
か、（墓碑パルコの縁辺に薄日さすことのまれまれ?）、他日たしかめ
ようとしてめぐりめぐってみたけれどむなしく、ただ、どこか高所のよ
うに、雪けむりたつ音の産生のまぼろしが放たれていたのだったか、
揺れに揺れて

（憩う間際に）
あるときはひとすじに読まれうる
独歩住居跡
またあるときはきれぎれに
国、木、田
住居
跡
独歩、歩
あふれ
（微風そのうらに名の剥落は尽き）

まるで、それらいくつかの漢字がたがいに離接や連接を繰り返しなが
ら、ついにみずからの根源を消去しようとしているかのような、（だれ
の脳の中にもない外にもない）、彷徨だ彷徨、しかし何にせよそれは
読まれるのだから、それはすでにみずからの成り立ちの外に出ている
というのに、同時にまた、読まれえない痕跡の過剰の中に消えてもい
るのだから、すなわちまだ、みずからの成り立ちの内にとどまってい
るという

（杭、この未知なるもの）
そのまわりを

3 (at half liberty)

(Ah, nothing but a single post marks the spot)
a voice once launched into an airspace
an airspace I still
fervently read at
the site of Doppo's lodge
(on hungry stones in dirt between infinitesimal city blocks)

in other words, what's called a vacant lot, where they'll dump a
high-rise, over each excited particle of the exposed clod, browning
in winter sun, I wonder if it was at the periphery of Tumulus
Emporium in Shibuya, (how curiously pale rays limn the Tombstone
Emporium), which in vain I perambulated later only to confirm, as
though glimpsed from far above, that nothing is transmitted but the
sound of phantom snowdust, blown back and forth, perhaps

(edged with stillness)
sometimes read in one breath
the site of Doppo's lodge
at other times in staccato
kuni 国 land, *ki* 木 tree, *da* 田 field,
lodge
site
as Doppo steps out alone
beyond
(names exfoliate in a back-eddy of breeze)

as if these kanji only iterate reciprocal disjunctions and conjunctions,
and finally extirpate their own roots, (not inside not outside of
nobody's brain), drift yes drift, but they are read in any case, and
so step beyond their own structure, and yet at the same time, they
dissolve in the excess of illegible traces, and so they abide inside their
own structure

(a single stela—the unknown)
its circumference
can be circled

81

たとえいまはぐるぐるとまわる
まわるしかないとしても
まなざしは興奮し
彷徨だ彷徨
（光芒またも組み合わさるだろう動不動の泥のへりへそ）

but even in circling
an ardor fills the gaze
drift yes drift
(Lightbeams will interlace again over the mud's shifting, shiftless edge
    and depth)

4（古バージョン）

それは、危機に満ち、
危機を、そして、
――かがやき、麗しの肌！
まだ見ぬ海の水際の泡、
のように、さきへさきへと、
行かせ、待機させ、
多岐にわたらせながら、
その折れた、逸れた、ひとつの系の、
とりあえずは南下だ、炎熱の、
浮く脂、環状線、
――視線、まぶしの色！
まだ見ぬ海？ いや、海はすでに、
しぶく後背の稜、その昏い波の飛沫に、
それを、その、
秘匿と、散逸と、
ともに反復しているのかもしれず、
反復はそして、まれな、
木の葉うらのそよぎ、不安な耳殻、
ましてうつつの霧を吹く地名の高み、
らをつたい、たえず、
たえず、ずれてゆくものだから、
――ゆびさき、踊るゆうべ！
歩むんだ、きょくたんに歩むんだ、
と復唱のしじまのひだを、
それは、文字の初期、
老いる風にまぎれて、
こちら側、足ひとつの統辞の、
側へと、送り返されている、
のかもしれず、点々と闇や、
ちいさな旋風の溜まり場を、
逸れ、危難に、
それは、未知、
と書かれ、消されている、
今一度、
水は水へ昏れてゆくあたりへと。

4 (old version)

It is, spiked with danger,
over danger, and,
—sparkling, ravishing skin!
going and going, like foam
at the edge of an unfathomed sea,
given to wash forward, to hold,
and to sprawl across its range,
across this eccentric, aberrant, system,
let's aim south first, blazing,
afloat in grease, along the loop line
—gazing, in a dazzle of color!
at the unfathomed sea? No, already the sea,
edges into its back-splash, into the dismal, breaker spray,
with its hiddenness,
and its dissipation,
or repetition of both,
and then the wheeling shifts, how strange,
to a rustling behind tree leaves, alarmed earshells,
and the peak of the place-name where awareness fogs over,
so leading, incessantly, forward
and, incessantly deviating, going toward,
—fingertips, an evening of dance!
walk to the extreme limit, walk,
so the recitation slides into the folds of a quietude,
it is an incunabula of ideograms,
stashed in the waning breeze,
sent back, perhaps, to this
side, the side of
a limping syntax, averting
dots of darkness,
and whirlpools,
hazards, where *unknown* is written,
and erased,
once again,
going toward, water twilights into water.

5（ダッダッダッダッ）

それ、独歩、うすい、
非常に住居跡、うすい、ので、
濃い、それでないもの、とのへり、
歩、へりを、つねに越えながら、
なお、非常に跡、とどまっているという、
そんなそれ、跡、へりに、
名、居させ、
名、住まわせよ、
国と木と、木と田と、田と微細と、
追うように、非常に名、這い、
歩、住居、追われるように、
それ、矛盾めく、微妙なすきまを、
這い、ねじれ、跡、
交叉し、歩、絡みあい、
それ、住居跡、うすい、
ただ、その不在によって在る、かのよう、
その欠如によって、跡、過剰、
かのよう、そんなそれ、非常に跡、
うすい、独歩、それ、

5 (daddaddadda)

it is, barely there, Doppo's
lodge very, barely there, and so,
hedged with, its contraries, heavy,
steps, constantly crossing, its threshold,
still, a vestige, remains,
such that, a sight of the site, bordered,
named, edged with light,
named, lodge site,
Land and Tree, Tree and Field, Field and the Infinitesimal,
as if in extreme, pursuit, the name, crawls,
steps clear of, the lodge, as if pursued,
in the dialectic, the infinitesimal chink,
there, crawls, twists, the traces,
cross-hatch, the steps, intertwine,
it is, the lodge site, barely there,
as if, just, to prevail over its perishing,
by virtue of its dearth, effaced, by excess,
as if, such that, the very trace,
is barely there, Doppo, it is,

6（威厳をもって、ひきずらぬように）

でさ、反復反復、反復彷徨
したんだけど、——

　　　　　　　反復はそして、まれな、
　　　　　　　木の葉うらのそよぎ、不安な耳殻、
　　　　　　　ましてうつつの霧を吹く地名の高み、
　　　　　　　らをつたい、たえず、
　　　　　　　たえず、ずれてゆくものだから、——

　　　　　　　　　　空域空域
　　　　　　　　　　空域一体
　　　　　　　　　　何故一体
　　　　　　　　　　空域彷徨

　　　　　　　　　　　　　　這い
振じれシティ、工場跡からは白髪のリア王がさまよい出る、這い振じ
れ突きたちシティ、野外劇の水臭い欄外で江戸の痕跡が跳ねる、這
い振じれ突きたち絡みあいシティ、理科系の後背地では夏草の寡黙
なゴーストダンスだ、這い振じれ突きたち絡みあい倦みシティ、幾星
霜の肌たちは灌木の茂みで耳の灰のような固有名の音をきく、——

　　　　　　　　　　独歩一体
　　　　　　　　　　一体彷徨
　　　　　　　　　　何故何故
　　　　　　　　　　彷徨独歩

　　　　　待って、あなたの痕跡、
　　　　　あなたの痕跡に、わたし、絡みあい倦み、——

這い
這い振じれ
這い振じれ交叉し
這い振じれ突きたち交叉し絡みあい
這い振じれ突きたち逸れ交叉し絡みあい倦み
　　　　　　　　　　倦み絡みあ
　　　　　　　い交叉し逸れ突きたち振じれ這い

88

6 (lightly, with ceremony)

and so, it's as though I'm
wheeling wheeling, wheeling adrift,—

      and then the wheeling shifts, how strange,
      to a rustling behind tree leaves, alarmed earshells,
      and the peak of the place-name where awareness fogs over,
      so leading, incessantly, forward
      and, incessantly deviating, going toward,—

                    Airspace Airspace
                    Earthly airspace
                    Earthly how so
                    Drift through airspace

                    In the crawly, wriggling city,
a white-haired Lear wanders from a vacant factory, slithering along,
wriggling through the rigid city, through the slip-slop margins of a
pageantry in which the imprint of Old Edo comes clear, wriggling,
crawling, rigid, weary, ensnared in the back beat of science and
engineering, where summer grasses dance a taciturn ghost dance, in the
wriggling, crawling, rigid, ensnared city, in a thicket of shrubs where the
flesh of epochs absorbs the sounds of place-names as ears absorb ashes,—

                    Doppo earthly
                    Earthly drifting
                    How so how so
                    Doppo drifting

      stay, imprint of my beloved,
      imprint of my beloved, I am, ensnared and weary of,—

crawl
crawltwist
crawltwistcross
crawltwisterectcrossinterlace
crawltwisterectdeviatecrossinterlacewear

絡みあい交叉し突きたち捩じれ這い

　　　　　　　　　　　交叉し捩じれ這い
　　　　　　　　　　　　　　捩じれ這い

　　　　独歩住居跡のほうへ
　　　　住居
　　　　跡
　　　　独歩、のほうへ、「行け、濡れた目
　　　　のなかを、──」

　　　　　　　反復反復　　反復彷徨
　　　　　　　空域一体　　彷徨彷徨

wearinterl
acecrossdeviateerecttwistcrawl

interlacecrosserecttwistcrawl

crosstwistcrawl
twistcrawl

On the way to the site of Doppo's lodge,
lodge
site
toward, Doppo, going, *through*
brimming eyes,—

wheeling wheeling wheeling adrift
earthly airspace adrift adrift

7（きわめて歌うように）

無限にそこ
指の多岐でたどるように
固有名はひしめき
そこ／無限に
そこ。

たとえば蛇が崩れ／とおく寂黙のうちに蛇が崩れ／ちらめく無性の幾
何が崩れて／その遺骸うるうると川となり／その遺骸うるうると川とな
り／川はほそまり川は隠れて／街々へ街のうらすじ街のへりへそ／そ
のみどり／その酷薄の美登利がどこまでも横たわっている

無限にそこ／無限に
そこは越えられてあり
しかしなお無限にたどりつけないそこ／そこに
固有名はひしめき
焦慮は描く
舞う足跡の軽やかな群れ
群れ。

あるいは泡を編むようにして
何の残響／何の
音の産生のまぼろし
とおく蛇は崩れ
酷薄の美登利は横たわっている

たおやかとはいえないだろうその背のラインに沿って
かわすか
そこ／かわされる
だろうそこ。

さらに足跡の群れ
きわめて歌うように
狂暴に
あるいはきわめて葬列のように。

7 (molto contabile)

Infinitely there
to be traced by branching fingers
a throng of place-names
there/ infinitely
there.

As for instance a rockslide serpentines/ in the distance silently
serpentines/ glimpse of brute geometry serpentines/ spilling its slough
into a river/ spilling its slough into a river /the river narrowing the
river dipping under/ the city's edge and depth the green/ Midori
enviously stretches out forever

Infinitely there, infinitely
there though surpassed
and infinitely inaccessible/ there
a throng of place-names
apprehension delineates
flocks of feathery footprints dancing
in flocks.

Or as if foam were stitched together
what reverberations/ what
but the sound of phantom snowdust
in the distance a rockslide serpentines
Midori enviously stretches out

along the curve of spine not willowy enough
to sidestep
there/ or there
to be given the slip.

And yet another flock of footprints
molto cantabile
furioso
or molto funebre.

8（歳時記とともに）

そこ
無限にそこ／そこにまるで
ひとつの固有名でも隠れているというように
無限に繰り返されるその指呼の波紋と
無限に躍動するそのにせの奥行きと
うつろ／うら
うら／うつつ
うつつ／うら
うら／うつろ
そこ。
むしろ歳時記をこそ。

たとえば水浅黄の空に
やがて卵色のやや濁った月がのぼるだろう
たまらなく夏の
そこ／あたりではまだ
犬のうすい舌のような紙に書かれた
真昼の書記のほてりが残っている
とはいえ／そこ
蝉しぐれもなく
みえない星の繭との出会いも無限にうすく抜け
さらなるインナー／その抜け抜けの旅へと
無限に蟻
無限にケンタウルス座アルファ
涼し。

青畝にせよ／波郷にせよ／独歩住居跡にせよ
涼し。

固有名とは
そのような無限
無限にそこ／そこへ
呼ぶひとの匿名の声の網が
とおく雨のようにやさしく降りかかりつつあり
涼し／あるいは片かげり
あら草に隠れるように

8 (with the calendar of season words)

There
infinitely there/ as if there
were a place-name hidden away
infinitely repeated, whose beckoning ripples-out and
infinitely agitated, whose simulacral depth
eddies/back
back/world
world/back
back/eddies
there.
So the season words if nothing else.

As, for instance, in the washed out azure sky
a hazy egg yolk moon will soon rise
unbearably summery
there/ lingering where
the swelter of midsummer's script is
written across paper thin as a puppy's tongue
nevertheless/ there
the shower of cidada chants dries up
the encounter between invisible stars and their cocoon fades infinitely,
dimming
into the deep/ into the exhausted journey
infinitely ants
infinitely Alpha Centauri
cooling off.

Either the poet Seiho/or Hakyô/or Doppo's lodge
cooling off.

Each place-name stands for
this kind of infinitude
infinitely there/ there
where a net of anonymous voices
showers down like distant rain
cooling off/ or on the shadow-side

未知へ／未知からの
無限にその固有名の崩壊の余韻のただなかを行く
そこ
無限にそこ。

as though hidden away in wild rushes
from the unknown/ to the unknown
infinitely abiding through the reverberations of that place-name's
        implosion
there
infinitely there.

9（コーダ、無の）

その、
無限にそこ、

そこに固有名はすみれのように折り畳まれて、
いつ、いつ開く、
と問われていたのでしたか、

その、
無限にそこ、

無限にそこに到り着こうとする、舞う軽やかな足跡は、
あらかじめ失われています、
あらかじめ失われています、

その、
無限にそこ、

その梁、その語らいの跡、
その遺伝子の芥、その庇、
その灌木の茂み、――

その、
無限にそこ、

部分また部分でしょうか、畝また畝でしょうか、

そこに刻み込むべき固有名を、
せめてその痕跡を、――と思ううち、
私たちはまた越えられてゆきます、

その、無限にそこ。

9 (coda, of nothing)

It is,
infinitely there,

there the place-name folded like violet petals,
asked,
when— when would it open itself,

it is,
infinitely there,

infinitely attempting to arrive there, in the spackle of danced footprints,
already gone,
already gone,

it is,
infinitely there,

that beam, that afterglow of conversation,
the dust of those genes, that eave,
that thicket of shrubs,—

it is,
infinitely there,

is it one part after another, is it one ridge after another,

hoping for a place-name to be engraved there,
or for its trace at least,—
we are one after another overcome,

it is, infinitely there.

四

IV.

（自失のように）

自由というのは
保存がきかない
たえず乱費されるか
使いもしないままに失われてゆくか
どちらかだ
という **自失のように**
寒林に
入り日アダージェット
暗澹と

(like abstractedness)

liberty is
not preserved
but it is
either endlessly squandered
or it expires before use
like abstractedness
the sun sets adagietto
in gloom
into the wintry forest

（あるいは深淵）

笠井叡に

突然
いつも突然
踊るひとはそこにいる
まるでひとのかたちをした
深淵の浮上
のようだ
小根まわし
ほき
ほかにたとえようが
ない
いや深淵そのもの
踊るひとは踊りながら
何かを叫ぶ
その口が
深淵そのものだ
それからその下に
布波
気多
漏斗の底の光のたゆたいのような
白い喉がみえる
喉の下は
肉の闇
踊るひとはだから
肉の闇が喉にこみあげてくる
のだし
喉をやぶってあらわれるのはしかし
べつの肉かもしれない
のだし
せつない雌雄性の影のもと
それをサロメと名づけても
セラフィータ
鏡の性器
と名づけても

(or chasm)

for Kasai Akira

suddenly
always suddenly
the one dancing is there
as if
a chasm given the figuration of
person would demerge
unrooted
precipice
no other
but
chasm itself
the one dancing dances while
howling something
whose mouth
becomes chasm itself
and from its depth
Hoooha
Ketha
come clear like light flashing in the
funnel's tail
is his pale throat
within which lies
the darkness of flesh
from the dancing figure's warm skin
the darkness of flesh rises
up in his throat
or instead
tearing through the throat erupts
another kind of flesh
perhaps
under the sign of heartrending
(fe)male-ness
whether we name it Salome

もはや自由であろう
　　　　　　　どころか
　喉を経て肉の闇は
　　　　　　きらきらした言葉に変わるかもしれない
　　　のだし
　　　　　　それを詩と呼んでも
　　　　銀河
　　　　　計画
　　　と呼んでも
　　　　　　もはや自由であろう
　　踊るひとはだから
　　　　　　それらすべてを
深淵がひきずりまわしてゆく
　　　　　　　　多々泥
　　　きらきらしい

Seraphita

or

the mirrored genitalia

no longer matters

on the contrary

the darkness of flesh

beyond the throat

may be transformed into sparkling

words

and

whether we call it poetry

or

Galaxy

Project

does not matter any longer

from the warm skin of the

one dancing

the chasm will drag

everything out

into the muddy sparkling

nebula

眼底ロード

私たちって誰だろう、
なぞなぞみたいだけれど、
夜通しあなたの眼底を旅してめぐるのが、
私たちの仕事、

道野辺には、
昼間のあなたの愚行の痕跡がまだ残っていて、
それを足の裏でスキャンしながら読み取ってゆく、
楽しい、

眼底の最も奥深いところには、
駄洒落みたいだけど、
あなたの苦悩が結晶してできた瑪瑙がごろごろしていて、
それを拾って叩きあわせ、
散った火花を写真に撮って、
夢見のあなたに送る、
楽しい、
楽しい、

もちろん、
朝が来るまでに、
音もなく私たちは立ち去る、
なぞなぞみたいだけれど、
そんな私たちって、
あなたにとって誰だろう、

Eyeground Road

who are we,
although this sounds like a riddle,
whose work it is to trek all night,
around your eye-grounds,

on the roadside,
where afterimages of the stupid things you do by day,
are scanned and read on the soles of our feet,
what a pleasure,

but in the depths of the eye-ground,
this may sound like a bad pun,
your agonies crystallize into pieces of agates that dot the road,
we pick them up and click them against each other,
to photograph the scattering sparks,
and send them to you in dreams,
what a pleasure,
what a pleasure,

naturally,
when morning breaks at last,
we silently withdraw,
this may sound like a riddle,
but what are we,
for you,

（凩）

今宵（くるみ）のような
小さな欲情を（俺）らは許して
歩むんだきょくたんに
おお∞今宵黄金の足さきに
獣の足跡めく斑紋が闇よりも濃く
点々と降りてきてそれは吉兆
見なれた常緑木の風景のなかに
ひそむ鳥のくびもその√
ひとさらいの出没する薄い林の境も
すべて（凩）の夜をついての
時ならぬピクニックめいて
ひとしきり仮睡をとれば
はやくもささくれだつ冬の根のさきに
見えないがつるむ猫たち
わけてもほそいほそい街道の（絹）の
その√の尽きるあたりで（俺）ら
まるで井戸をのぞき込むよう
何の芝居の埃立つ擬斗であろうか
（死児）として丸まり昇ってくる男たちを
ひとりずつすくいあげては（俺）ら
キックするあるいはされる
気がつくと黒々と梁の交差する廃屋に捉えられ
底光りする石胎のうえで
死んだ（火）の√の鼻さきとの
むかしの愛のおさらい
あるいはさらに山深くわけ入り
なおも行きまよう足さきは
黄金から灰へのその苦い（私註）のように
おお∞棕櫚一本の自生

(draft)

tonight (I) and (I) admit
to a little lust like (a walnut)
and walk martially
tonight oh ∞ on gilded toes
as speckles like the footprints of a beast thick as darkness
drip into an augury
in a landscape of familiar evergreens
the birds with their √ necks stalk
along thinning edges of the kidnapper-haunted forest
all reminiscent of an untimely picnic
through the (drift)y night
after a short doze
with winter's root-tips splitting already
and cats though invisible carousing
on the particularly narrow narrow road's (silk)
where its √ diminishes (I) and (I)
as though peeping into a well
what do we see if not some staged combat
where one by one men are scooped out
who (as stillborns) bounce upward in balls that (I) and (I)
kick or am kicking all of (my) and (my)selves
caught in a derelict house its black beams exposed
in a stone uterus dark and glistening
a rehearsal for some long gone romance
with the muzzle of the dead (fire)'s √
or pushing deeper yet into the mountains
(my) feet meandering
from gold to ash annotated as bitter (marginalia) like
oh ∞ a windmill-palm growing alone

（あるいは豚小屋）

鳥籠に春が、春が鳥のゐない鳥籠に。
三好達治

豚小屋に春が、
春が豚のゐない豚小屋に、
その床に私の足跡が、
足跡にかすかな塵が、
その塵が、
舞う、
舞う、

生きることを休みたい？ 苦しい私を取り替えたい？ 馬鹿な、そんな私を掘り下げよ、深く、深く、すると筋肉のように不穏な、朽ちかけた豚小屋にふれる、母よ、彼岸へと脳の梁を伸ばしつつある母よ、掘り下げることがすでに豚小屋である、筋肉が不穏にうごめくならば、それ自体がすでに豚小屋である、だってほら、すでにあふれかえるほどの勢いで、おのれ自身を覆い隠すほどに、**あれ**がみえているではないか、だから働け、遊べ、豚小屋に豚がいるとはかぎらない、キーキーと安っぽい叫びをあげながら去勢されている**あれ**は誰か、涙がきらめき、草が萌え、終わりのない幼年、終わりのない泥濘、やがて糞尿の臭いよりも強烈な光に覆われるなかで、なおもキーキーと安っぽい叫びをあげながら去勢されている**あれ**は誰か、母よ、私の消去をなせ、彼岸へと脳の梁を伸ばしつつある母よ、私の消去をなせ、梁の下で、まだ聞こえるキーキー、蒸されたばかりの隣接の茶の葉が夥しく、舞う、すべては舞う、板が立てられ、また板が立てられ、

舞う、
舞う、
前が後ろになったり、
右が左になったり、
板々しい、あるいは豚小屋、
豚小屋に春が、
春が豚のゐない豚小屋に、

(or pigsty)

To the birdcage comes spring, spring to the birdless birdcage.
—Miyoshi Tatsuiji

to the pigsty comes spring,
spring to the pigless pigsty,
on its floor my footstep,
on my footstep a macula of dust,
and the dust,
swirling,
swirling,

want a break from life? want to quit the suffering I? forget it, it's
better to root deeper, deeper into the I to reach the crumbling pigsty,
ominously muscular, dear mother extending the beam of your mind
to the far shore, sweet mother, the act of rooting is, itself, pigsty, and
if the muscles quiver, that too is pigsty, as you see, in the surging
momentum, which almost overcomes your self, WHICH IS WHAT
begins to come clear, so work hard, play hard, a pigsty doesn't always
hide a pig, WHICH IS WHAT, as it's castrated, squeaks profane
squeaks, tears sparkling, grass shooting up, in endless infancy, in
endless mire, until it's slathered in light more intense than the reek of
nightsoil, WHICH IS WHAT, as it's castrated, continues to squeak
profane squeaks, dear mother, remove me, sweet mother extending
the beam of your mind to the far shore, remove me, under the beam,
the squeaking persists, a big dollop of the adjacent freshly steamed
tea-leaves, whirling, all whirling, a plank is placed, another plank,

whirling,
whirling,
front becomes back,
right becomes left,
painboards, or pigsty,
to the pigsty comes spring,
spring to the pigless pigsty

（夜ごと私たちは連れていかれる）

夜ごと　私たちは連れていかれる
誰もいない場所に　誰も生じえない場所に
愛する者にお別れをいうまもなく
とりどりの子供たちの鬼面が　迎えに来るのだ

途中　さびれた街なかを抜け
いくつかの橋を渡るが
下を川が流れているようには思えない
むしろ草　夜の低みのみだらな草

ああ私たちは　そこに欲望を解消することもできたのに
また途中　子供たちのひとりが
鬼面を脱ぎ　向こうには雪が欠けている
時の湯垢のように降る雪が
と忠告するけれど

その顔も　街の灯のように遠ざかる
愛する大地　愛する大地
それから不意に　私たちは中空にせり出してゆく
かのよう　眼は取り払われて

眼は取り払われて
どこをどう経めぐったのか
気がつくと　みえないが
誰もいない場所だ　誰も生じえない場所だ

私たちは淋しいし
耳からひるひる分身を躍り出させて
互いが互いの影を撫でるように　たたずむ
そのとき　そこにいるのは誰だ

そこにいるのは誰だ　と二度
厳しく問われてしまう
その声のほうへ　私たちはしかし
昏れてゆくことができない

(nightly we are taken)

nightly   we are taken
to the place no one goes   the place no one arrives
without farewell to those we love
the myriad devil masks of children   come for us

on our way   through a desolate town
we cross serial bridges
and beneath them flow rivers only
of weeds   wanton weeds, night's low-lying land

ah we might have   drained our desires there
and when we're on our way again   one of the children
peels off his devil mask   to warn us
that the snow here drifting down like time's limescale
thins out to nothing on the other side

and then even his face   fades like city light
my sweet old earth   my sweet old earth
with no warning   we are upthrust into midair
or so it seems   our eyes plucked out

our eyes plucked out
where and how it comes about
we can't presume   but now we are here
in the place no one goes   the place—no one arrives

we are so desolate
our fluttering doubles leap from our ear
as if to caress each other's shadow   we stand stock still
and right then   who's there?

who's there?   twice
the question is barked
but because we cannot gloam
back at the voice

夜ごと　だから私たちは戻ってくるのだ
いくつかの橋を渡り　濡れて大きな
泣きはらしたような眼を
嵌められて

nightly therefore   we return
recrossing serial bridges   enchased with
big wet eyes swollen
with weeping

コーダ

街の、衣の、
いちまい、下の、
虹は、蛇だ、
街の、衣の、
いちまい、(meta) の、
蛇は、虹だ、
かすか、呼気、カーブして、
青く、呼気、カーブして、
わたくしは、葉に、揉まるる、
葉は、水に、揉まるる、
街の、衣の、いちまい、下の、虹は、蛇だ、
蛇の、粋の、いちまい、横の、声は、ヨーガだ、蛇の、
粋の、いちまい、(para) の、ヨーガは、声だ、声の、筋の、
いちまい、上の、景は、さやぐ、声の、筋の、いちまい、(poly) の、
景も、さやぐ、景を、あら敷き、結合の、きゃっ、添え、膜を、あら敷き、
分泌の、ひゃっ、添え、ふささ、さむ、衣の、にぎ夢、ひたた、たむ、衣の、
ざざ夢、ららら、ひとの穂、飛ぶよ、ららら、ひとの腑、浮くよ、街の、
衣の、いちまい、下の、虹は、蛇だ、蚶だ、蚯だ、蚫だ、蛔だ、
蛟だ、蜒だ、らむ、だむ、そよぎ、だむ、たむ、さわぎ、
蚶だ、蚯だ、きゃっ、ぎゃっ、きゃみ、髪、神、
街の、衣の、いちまい、下の、虹は、蛇だ、
わたくしは、葉に、揉まるる、
葉は、水に、揉まるる、
かすか、呼気、カーブして、
青く、呼気、カーブして、
街の、衣の、
いちまい、(meta) の、
蛇は、虹だ、
街の、衣の、
いちまい、下の、
虹は、蛇だ、

118

Coda

one layer, below,
the city's, slough,
there's a rainbow, snake,
one layer, (meta) to,
the city's, slough,
there's a snake, rainbow,
faint, breath, and curves,
blue, breath, and curves,
I'm, kneaded, by leaves,
leaves, kneaded, in water,
one layer, below, the city's, slough, is a rainbow, snake,
one layer, close to, the snake's, elegance, is a voice, yoga, one layer,
(para) to, the snake's, elegance, is yoga, a voice, one layer, above,
the voice's, sinew, is a panorama, moaning, one layer, (poly) to, the voice's,
                                                                          sinew,
is a view, also moaning, to the spread-eagled, panorama, a conjunctive, phew,
is affixed, to the spread-eagled, membrane, a secretious, whew,
is affixed, swishing, tassels, are a trousseau's brustling, dreams, shirred, fold, are
dreasy dreams, la-la-la, human tassels, dehisce, la-la-la, human viscera, float,
                                                                          one layer,
below, the city's, slough, is a rainbow, snake, lizard, gecko, dragon, abalone,
arkshell, rainworm, wham, bang, whir, clang, damn, warble,
lizard, gecko, gowee, goo, gads, gob, god,
one layer, below, the city's, slough, is a rainbow, snake,
I'm, kneaded, by leaves,
leaves, kneaded, in water,
faint, breath, and curves,
blue, breath, and curves,
one layer, (meta) to,
the city's, slough,
is a snake, rainbow,
one layer, below,
the city's, slough,
is a rainbow, snake,

119

わたくしはニットを編む 第弐番
（幸福物質経路）

わたくしはニットを編む
ぜがひでも編む
生きてあることの
刻々の結節を認めない
いつもすべすべの
瑪瑙のような眼の裏のおぞましさ
そこが幸福物質経路
さらに内奥の
ひたぶるにうららな襞に至り
暗き者ふたたび胎の者らが群れて
光すらしわくちゃにむなしい
そこが幸福物質経路
女たちは言う
犬を飼いたかったから
あるいは苗字に惹かれて
それがとりあえず結婚に踏み切る理由
生きてあることの
葉も端も
歯やシャーベットほどには輝かず
ところどころ
ひと型の水滴が
無い生まれたてのへこみや突起を
まさぐっているけれどみえない
そこが幸福物質経路
子供たちは言う
寝るまえの自分と
起きたあとの自分と
ぴったり重なるとはかぎらない
わたくしはニットを編む
ぜがひでも編む
記憶にない賑わいの格子を絡めて
消えてゆく道という道
無い生まれたての

I am Knitting, No. 2
(felicity substance channel)

I'm knitting
just knitting away
denying every minute's knot
its chance to live
always clear as agate
the horror behind the eye
where felicity's substance passes
deeper into the guts
of the intensely serene folds
dark beings twice-uterine beings throng
where the light crinkles futilely
where felicity's substance passes
some women say
because I wanted a dog
or was drawn to his last name
which is how from the start they plunge into marriage
neither the leaves nor edges
of living presence
gleam as much as teeth or sherbet
here and there
beads of water take on human shapes
groping at fresh pits and nubs that don't yet exist
invisible as they are
where felicity's substance passes
some children say
the I before going to bed
and the I upon waking
don't necessarily match up
I'm knitting
just knitting away
snarls in the merry latticework I can't remember
all paths disappear
leaving behind

へりは残して
とその左右から
叢林が突然に明るく
ちらばる脂
つらなる耳
その朵にひそやかな出血があったりして
そこが幸福物質経路
さらにその左右から
誰をも容れない廃屋のような繭が
つぎつぎと立ちならび燃えあがりくずおれてゆく
巫女の衣装のように
燃えあがり
くずおれてゆく
果ては雪の夕暮れ
わたくしはニットを編む
ぜがひでも編む

the fresh edge that doesn't yet exist
from which from left and right
the thicket turns suddenly bright
its fat spattering
its ears strung up
some branches weakly bleeding
where felicity's substance passes
further off to the left and right
cocoons like inaccessible vacant houses
are lined up one behind the other in flames and crumbling
the way Sibyl's regalia
goes up in flames
and crumbles
beyond lies the snowy evening
I'm knitting
just knitting away

ロマンス

ぼくがもとめる幸福は単純だ
一度かぎりの潮のように
午後のおだやかな暑熱をひらき
きみとともにあること
そうではないそうですらない
ぼくがもとめる幸福は単純だ
午後のおだやかな暑熱がおのずから
繰り返し繰り返しひらかれてあること
そのひらかれの果てでぼくがもう
きみについてさえ何も思い出せないとき
それでもそのとき陽を浴びている石があること
石は記憶よりも暑いし数えられるから
ぼくがもとめる幸福は単純だ
浮かんでは消えてゆく自然数の
はるか右上に瑪瑙?　そう瑪瑙のような
空の葉の硬いさわさわが感じられ
そのさわさわがなおも翻りそうな予感のなか
ぼくがもとめる幸福は単純だ
なぜならそのとき砧骨にも蕾が発生して
砧骨にも蕾が発生して

Romance

The happiness I hope for is simple
like a tide that comes only once
opening the tranquil swelter of afternoon
and to be with you
no that's not it that's not quite it
the happiness I hope for is simple
the tranquil afternoon swelter naturally
and over and over and over opens itself
at the end of its openness I no longer
recall anything about you
despite that at the moment a stone soaks in the sun
since stones can be counted and get hotter than memory
the happiness I hope for is simple
far to the right of appearing and disappearing natural numbers
is that an agate? yes something like an agate
and a fricative rustling of the sky's leaves can be felt
even as the rustling feeling flutters diminishing
the happiness I hope for is simple
because at the moment a flower bud pops open in my inner ear
on my stapes a flower bud pops open

Biographical Notes

Kyoko Yoshida was born and raised in Fukuoka, Japan. She has a Ph.D. from the University of Wisconsin-Milwaukee, and she was a participant of the 2005 International Writing Program at University of Iowa. Her stories have been published in *The Massachusetts Review, Chelsea,* and *The Beloit Fiction Journal,* among other places. She is working on a novel about the visit of American Negro League baseball players to Japan in the 1930's. In addition, she translates Japanese contemporary poetry and drama. Recently a Visiting Scholar at Brown University, she teaches English at Keio University and lives in Yokohama.

Forrest Gander's recent books include the novel *As a Friend,* the book of poems *Core Samples from the World,* and the translation *Firefly Under the Tongue: Selected Poems of Coral Bracho* (PEN Translation Prize Finalist). A United States Artists Rockefeller Fellow, Gander is recipient of fellowships from the NEA, the Guggenheim, Howard, and Whiting foundations. He is the Adele Kellenberg Seaver Professor of Literary Arts and Comparative Literature at Brown University.

Spectacle & Pigsty
by Kiwao Nomura

Cover text set in Bernard Modern Standard & Adobe Garamond Pro.
Interior text set in Adobe Kozuko Mincho Pro, Adobe Kozuko
Gothic Pro, Bernard Modern Standard & Adobe Garamond Pro.

Book offset printed by Thomson-Shore, Inc., Dexter, Michigan
on Glatfelter Natures Natural 60# archival quality recycled paper
to the Green Press Initiative standard.

Cover art by K. Ruby Blume
Lichen Masks, ceramic, photograph by K. Ruby Blume

Cover and interior design by Ken Keegan.

Omnidawn Publishing
Richmond, California
2011

Ken Keegan & Rusty Morrison, Co-Publishers & Senior Editors
Cassandra Smith, Poetry Editor & Book Designer
Sara Mumolo, Poetry Editor & Poetry Features Editor
Gillian Hamel, Poetry Editor & Senior Blog Editor
Jared Alford, Facebook Editor
Peter Burghardt, Bookstore Outreach Manager
Juliana Paslay, Bookstore Outreach & Features Writer
Craig Santos Perez, Media Consultant